Sheet Music
for Album No. 1

Your Eyes Have Told Me Everything

Music Scores & Lyrics in English & in Chinese
for the Love Songs by Gang Chen Series

Gang Chen

ArchiteG®, Inc.
Irvine, California

Sheet Music for Album No. 1, Your Eyes Have Told Me Everything*: Music Scores & Lyrics in English & in Chinese for the Love Songs by Gang Chen Series*

Copyright © 2013 Gang Chen
V1.1   Issued on 1/16/2014
Cover Photo © 2013 Gang Chen

Copy Editor: Penny L Kortje

ArchiteG®, Inc.
http://www.ArchiteG.com

ISBN: 978-1-61265-016-6

PRINTED IN THE UNITED STATES OF AMERICA

Dedication

To my parents, Zhuixian and Yugen,
my wife, Xiaojie, and my daughters,
Alice, Angela, Amy, and Athena.

Disclaimer

Sheet Music for Album No. 1, Your Eyes Have Told Me Everything is a collection of music scores and lyrics in English and Chinese for the *Love Songs by Gang Chen Series*. The book is sold with the understanding that neither the publisher nor the authors are providing legal, accounting, or other professional services. If legal, accounting, or other professional services are required, seek the assistance of a competent professional firm.

The purpose of this publication is to provide a valuable tool for people to learn, play, and sing these songs.

Great effort has been taken to make this resource as complete and accurate as possible. However, nobody is perfect and there may be typographical errors or other mistakes present. If you find any potential errors, please send an e-mail to:
info@ArchiteG.com

Sheet Music for Album No. 1, Your Eyes Have Told Me Everything is intended to provide general, entertaining, informative, educational, and enlightening content. Neither the publisher nor the author shall be liable to anyone or any entity for any loss or damages, or alleged loss or damages, caused directly or indirectly by the content of this book.

If you do not wish to be bound by the above, you may return this book to the publisher for a full refund.

Legal Notice

Love Songs by Gang Chen Series

Welcome to the music world of ArchiteG, Inc. We believe music belongs to people and not just the elite, and music of the people, by the people, for the people, shall not perish from the earth.

To this end, we create the *Love Songs by Gang Chen Series* to give you a unique music experience through our albums, singles, and books.

You can listen to the vocal version of our songs, or listen to a musical instrument simulating human voice, or you can actively participate and sing our songs over our Karaoke background music track albums.

All songs in our albums are brand-new original songs. Four versions of each song are included:
1. **English version** (Full English vocal with background music)
2. **Instrumental version** (Musical instrument simulating the human voice)
3. **Karaoke version** (Background music track for Karaoke singing or sing along)
4. **Chinese version (**Full Chinese vocal with background music)

We have also published a book of sheet music for each album to provide our fans with music score and lyrics in both English and Chinese. This provides a valuable tool for people to learn to play and sing our songs.

We believe many people will like or love our albums and books once they really know about them. Our biggest challenge now is to let as many people know about the book as possible. Please help us spread the word.

I have a small wish: to have everyone on the planet hear me sing or hear the songs I wrote or produced. I have included the instrumental version so that people who do not speak English or Chinese can use this version to learn the songs and sing in their native language.

All of our singles and albums are available at
Music.ArchiteG.com

All our books are available at
GreenExamEducation.com

How to Use This Book

We suggest you read *Sheet Music for Album No. 1, Your Eyes Have Told Me Everything* at least three times.

Read once to get a general idea of the book. Highlight the information you are not familiar with.

Read twice to learn how to play and sing each song, focusing on the highlighted information to memorize. You can repeat this process as many times as you want until you master each song.

Read for the final time the night before your performance, focusing on the information you highlighted.

This book is very light so you can easily carry it around. These features will allow you to review the songs whenever you have a few minutes.

The Table of Contents is very detailed so you can locate information quickly. If you are on a tight schedule you can forgo reading the book linearly and jump around to the sections you need.

Table of Contents

Chapter One   **Lyrics in English and in Chinese for Album No.1, Love Songs by Gang Chen Series**

Chapter Two   **Sheet Music for Album No.1, Love Songs by Gang Chen Series**

Appendixes

Chapter One

**Lyrics in English & in Chinese for
Album No.1, Love Songs by Gang Chen Series**

A Naughty Girl
一个淘气的女孩

Lyric and Music by Gang Chen
由陈钢作词和作曲

Many years ago I met a naughty girl
多年以前，我遇见了一个淘气的女孩
She says she wants to try everything in love
她说她想尝试爱的一切
She wants to love and be loved
她希望爱与被爱
She wants to abandon and be abandoned
她想抛弃与被抛弃
She wants to break some hearts and
她要伤别人的心
She wants her heart broken...
也希望别人伤她的心......

Many years ago I met a naughty girl
多年以前，我遇见了一个淘气的女孩
She says she wants to try everything in love
她说她想尝试爱的一切
She wants to love and be loved
她希望爱与被爱
She wants to abandon and be abandoned
她想抛弃与被抛弃
She wants to break some hearts and
她要伤别人的心
She wants her heart broken...
也希望别人伤她的心......

Naughty girl, naughty girl

淘气的女孩，淘气的女孩

If we ever meet again, will you still be so naughty?

如果我们再相见，你还会这么淘气吗？

Naughty girl, naughty girl

淘气的女孩，淘气的女孩

If we ever meet again, will you still be so naughty?

如果我们再相见，你还会这么淘气吗？

Naughty girl, naughty girl

淘气的女孩，淘气的女孩

If we ever meet again, will you still be so naughty?

如果我们再相见，你还会这么淘气吗？

Naughty girl, naughty girl

淘气的女孩，淘气的女孩

If we ever meet again, will you still be so naughty?

如果我们再相见，你还会这么淘气吗？

Circle of Love
爱情链

Lyric and Music by Gang Chen
由陈钢作词和作曲

I love you, you love him, he loves her, and she loves me...
我爱你，你爱他，他爱她，她爱我...
This is a circle of love
这是一个爱情链

When we are young, we are always looking for
当我们年轻的时候，我们一直在寻找
people we want to love, and we
我们要爱的人
do not know how to break this circle of love
不知如何打开这个爱情链

When we grow older, we start to appreciate
当我们渐渐长大，我们开始欣赏
people who love us
那些爱我们的人
We start to learn what true love is
开始了解什么是真正的爱情

I love you, you love him, he loves her, and she loves me...
我爱你，你爱他，他爱她，她爱我...
This is a circle of love
这是一个爱情链
Can we break this circle of love?
能否打开这个爱情链？

I love you, you love him, he loves her, and she loves me...
我爱你，你爱他，他爱她，她爱我...
This is a circle of love
这是一个爱情链
How do we break this circle of love?
如何打开这个爱情链？

I love you, you love him, he loves her, and she loves me...

我爱你，你爱他，他爱她，她爱我...

This is a circle of love

这是一个爱情链

Can we break this circle of love?

能否打开这个爱情链？

The past has become a beautiful memory
过去已经成为了美好的回忆

Lyric and Music by Gang Chen
由陈钢作词和作曲

I met a girl I used to know
我遇见了一位我曾相识的女孩
We talked about past, present, and future
我们谈论过去，现在和未来

She was laughing
她在欢笑
We were smiling
我们在微笑
Everything seemed to be perfect
一切似乎很完美

She has a beautiful family and
她有一个美丽的家庭
I have a wonderful life
而我也有美好的生活

I told her "the past has become a beautiful memory"
我告诉她："过去已变成美好的回忆"
All of a sudden she became so angry
突然之间，她变得如此生气
and I could not figure out why
我不知道为什么

Maybe she does not want to become a memory
或许她不想成为回忆
Maybe she wants to take over
也许她想永远占有
a corner of my heart forever...
我心灵一角......

Maybe she does not want to become a memory
或许她不想成为回忆
Maybe she wants to take over
也许她想永远占有
a corner of my heart forever...
我心灵一角......

I told her "the past has become a beautiful memory"
我告诉她："过去已变成美好的回忆"
All of a sudden she became so angry
突然之间，她变得如此生气
I cannot figure out why
我不知道为什么

Maybe she does not want to become a memory
或许她不想成为回忆
Maybe she wants to take over
也许她想永远占有
a corner of my heart forever...
我心灵一角......

Maybe she does not want to become a memory
或许她并不想成为回忆
Maybe she wants to take over
也许她想永远占有
a corner of my heart forever...
我心灵一角......

Is this love?
难道这就是爱？

Lyric and Music by Gang Chen
由陈钢作词和作曲

Is this love?
难道这就是爱？
Is this love?
难道这就是爱？

Why does my heart start pounding when I hear your name?
为何每当听见你名字就怦然心动？
Why do my eyes always search for you in the crowd?
为何我双眼总是在人群中搜寻你？
Why can't I look you straight in the eyes?
为何我不能直视你的眼？
Why do you always appear in my dreams?
为何你总是出现在我梦里？

Is this love?
难道这就是爱？
Is this love?
难道这就是爱？
Is this love?
难道这就是爱？
Is this love?
难道这就是爱？

Why does my heart start pounding when I hear your name?
为何每当听见你名字就怦然心动？
Why do my eyes always search for you in the crowd?
为何我双眼总是在人群中搜寻你？
Why can't I look you straight in the eyes?
为何我不能直视你的眼？
Why do you always appear in my dreams?
为何你总是出现在我梦里？

Is this love?
难道这就是爱？
Is this love?
难道这就是爱？

Do you really love me?
你真的爱我吗?

Lyric and Music by Gang Chen
由陈钢作词和作曲

"Do you really love me?"
"你真的爱我吗？"
"Do you really love me?"
"你真的爱我吗？"
"If you love me, why don't you seem to care about me?"
"如果你爱我，为什么你似乎并不在乎我？"
You always ask
你总是问

"If you love me
"如果你爱我
Why don't you seem to be afraid to lose me?"
为什么你似乎不怕失去我？"
You always ask
你总是问

"If you love me
"如果你爱我
Why don't you seem to be concerned about me?"
为什么你似乎不关心我？"
You always ask
你总是问

Well, my girl
哎，女孩
If you belong to me
如果你属于我
I do not need to be concerned
我并不需要担心

Well, my girl

哎，女孩

If you do not belong to me

如果你不属于我

I do not need to be concerned either

我也不需要担心

Well, my girl

哎，女孩

If you belong to me

如果你属于我

I do not need to be concerned

我并不需要担心

Well, my girl

哎，女孩

If you do not belong to me

如果你不属于我

I do not need to be concerned either...

我也不需要担心......

Your Eyes Have Told Me Everything
你的眼睛告诉了我一切

Lyric and Music by Gang Chen
由陈钢作词和作曲

Don't say anything
什么也别说
Don't say anything
什么也别说
Don't say anything
什么也别说
Your eyes have told me everything
你的眼睛告诉了我一切

Your hands are shaking
你的手在颤抖
My heart is pounding
我的心在砰砰的跳
and I love this feeling
我爱这种感觉

Don't say anything
什么也别说
Don't say anything
什么也别说
Don't say anything
什么也别说
Your eyes have told me everything
你的眼睛告诉了我一切

Your eyes are sparkling
每当你听我唱歌时
when you hear me singing
你的眼睛就泛起闪光
and I love this feeling
我爱这种感觉

Hey! Hey! 嘿！ 嘿！
Your eyes have told me everything
你的眼睛告诉了我一切

Don't say anything
什么也别说
Your eyes have told me everything...
你的眼睛告诉了我一切......

Swing
秋千

Lyric and Music by Gang Chen
由陈钢作词和作曲

The grass is green
草坪青翠
The sun is shining
阳光明媚
and you are sitting on a swing
你坐在那秋千上

The swing is flying
秋千在飞翔
and you are smiling
你在微笑

I love you, darling
我爱你，亲爱的
and we are smiling
我们在微笑

The swing is flying
秋千在飞翔
and you are smiling
你在微笑
and you are sitting on a swing
你坐在那秋千上

The swing is flying
秋千在飞翔
and you are smiling
你在微笑
and you are sitting on a swing...
你坐在那秋千上......

I Want It All as I Have Told You
我全都要，我早已告诉你

Lyric and Music by Gang Chen
由陈钢作词和作曲

I want it all as I have told you
我全都要，我早已告诉你
I want our memory
我要我们的回忆
I want your beauty
我要你的美丽
I want your love
我要你的爱

I want it all as I have told you
我全都要，我早已告诉你
I want our family
我要我们的家庭
I want our life
我要我们的生活
I want our future to be together
我要我们的未来

I want it all as I have told you
我全都要，我早已告诉你
I want it all as I have told you
我全都要，我早已告诉你
I want it all as I have told you...
我全都要，我早已告诉你......

Chapter Two

Sheet Music for Album No.1, Love Songs by Gang Chen Series

A Naughty Girl

(Melody)

Gang Chen

G   D   G7   G#dim

ab an don and to be ab an doned she wantto breaksomehearts and she wanther heart

Am6   A#dim   D7 Dmaj7 D Dadd9- G   Gaug

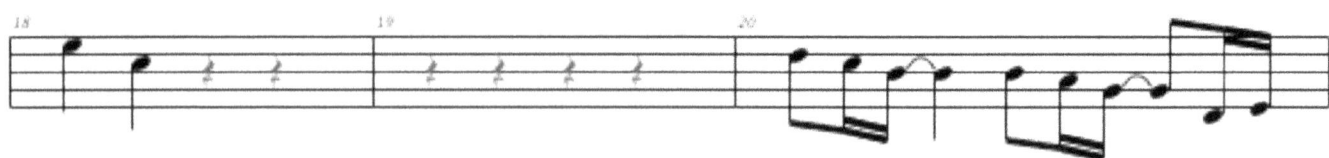

bro ken   Naughty girl Naughty girl if we

C   D7   G Gaug   C   D7

ev er meet ag ain will you still be so naugh   ty?

G   Gaug   C   D7   G   Gaug

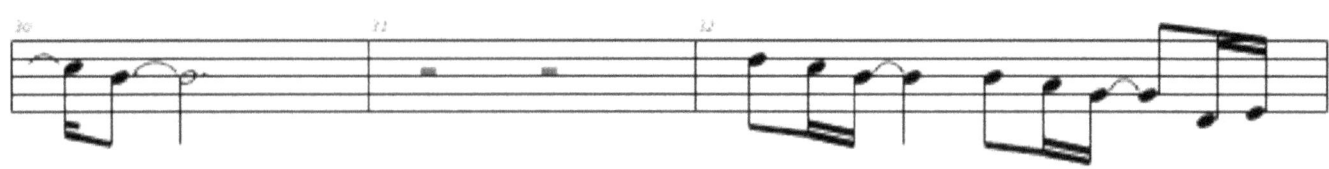

Naughty girl Naughty girl if we ev er meet ag ain will you still be so naugh   ty?

C D7   G   Gaug   C   D7

Naughty girl Naughty girl if we ev er meet ag ain will you still be so naugh

G   Gaug   C   D7   G   Gaug

ty?   Naughty girl Naughty girl if we

ev er meet ag ain will you still be so naugh ty?

Circle Of Love

(Melody)

Gang Chen

A#   C   A#   C   A#

she loves me   this is a   cir cle of   love

C   A#   G#   G   C

can we   break this cir cle of   lo   ve   I love you

A#   C   A#   C

you love him   he loves her and   she loves me   this is a

A#   C   A#   C   A#

cir cle of   love   how do we   break this cir cle of

G#   G

lo   ve   I love you   you love him   he loves her and

A#   C   A#   C

she loves me   this is a   cir cle of   love

Outro

C

can we   break this cir cle of   lo   ve

A#   C   A#

63   64   65   66   67   68

The Past Has Become A Beautiful Memory

(Melody)

Gang Chen

Fm — Eb — Db — C

May be she does not want to be come a mem o ry

Fm — Eb — Db

May be she wants to take ov er a cor ner of my heart for

C — Fm — Eb — Db

ev er I told her The past has be come a beau ti ful mem o ry

C — Fm — Eb — Db — C

All of a sud den she be came so an gry I can not fi gure out

C — Fm — Eb — Db — C

why May be she does not want to be come a mem o ry

Fm — Eb — Db — C

May be she want to take ov er a cor ner of my heart for ev er

Is This Love?

(Melody)

Gang Chen

C   Em   F

Is this   lo   o   o   o   ove?   Is this

C   F   Fm   C

love?   Why does my heart start   pounding   when   I   hear your   name?

E   Am

Why   do   my   eyes al   ways   search   for   you   in   the   crowd?

F   Fm   C

Why   cant   I   look you straight   in   the   eyes?   Why do   you al   ways ap pear in   my

E   F   Fm   C   C

dreams?   Is   this   love?   Is   this   love?   Is   this   lo   o

Em   F   C   F

o   o   ove?   Is   this   love?   Why does my heart start

Fm · C · E

35 / 36 / 37 / 38

pounding · when I hear your name? · Why do my eyes al ways

Am · F

39 / 40 / 41 / 42

search for you · in the crowd? · Why cant I look you straight

Fm · C · E · F

43 / 44 / 45 / 46

in the eyes? · Why do you al ways ap pear in my · dreams? Is this love?

Fm · C

47 / 48 / 49

Is this love?

Do You Really Love Me?

(Melody)

Gang Chen

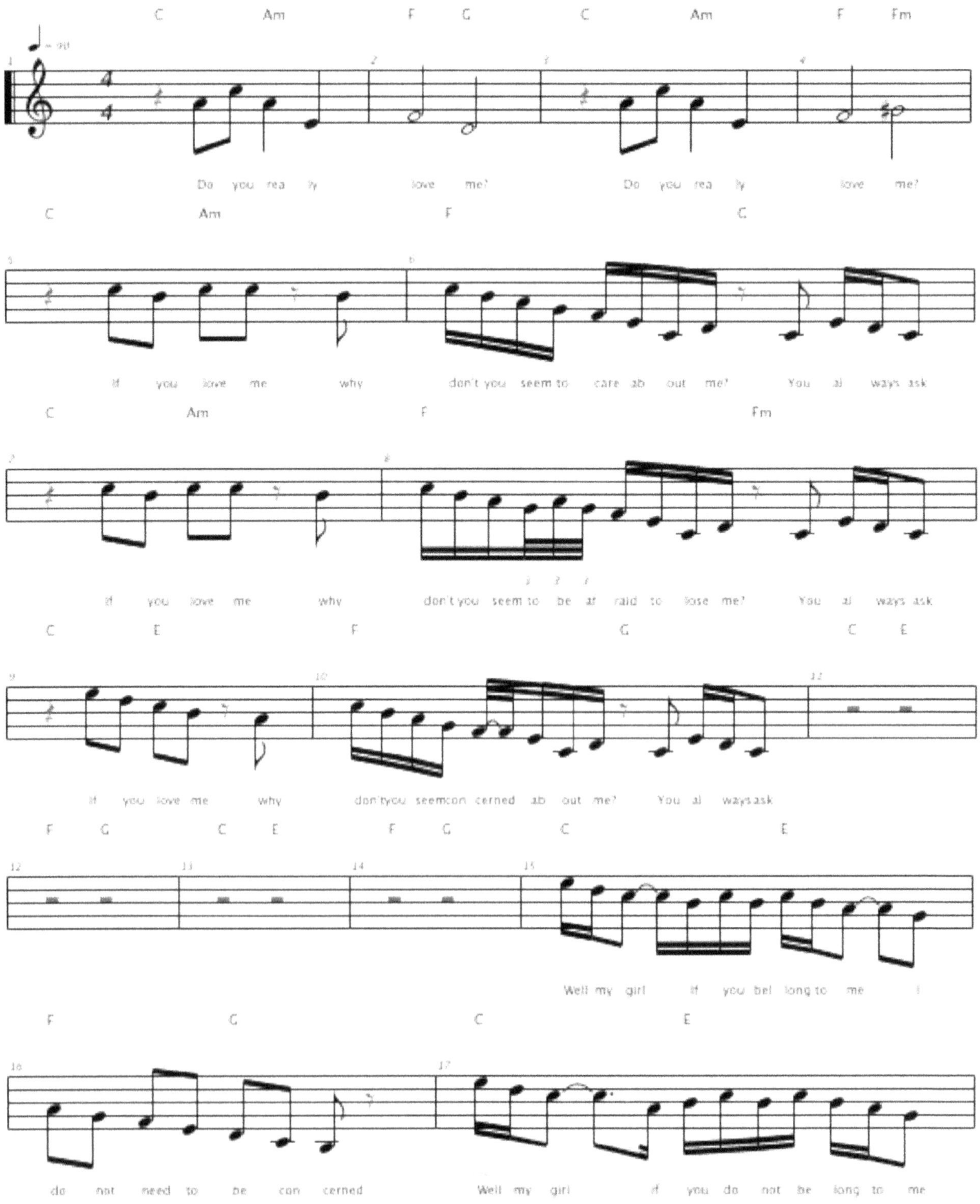

F   G   C   E

I don't need to be con cerned ei ther   Well my girl If you bel long to me   I

F   G   C   E

do not need to be con cerned   Well my girl if you do not be long to me

F   G   C

I don'tneedto be con cernei ther

Your Eyes Have Told Me Everything

(Melody)

Gang Chen

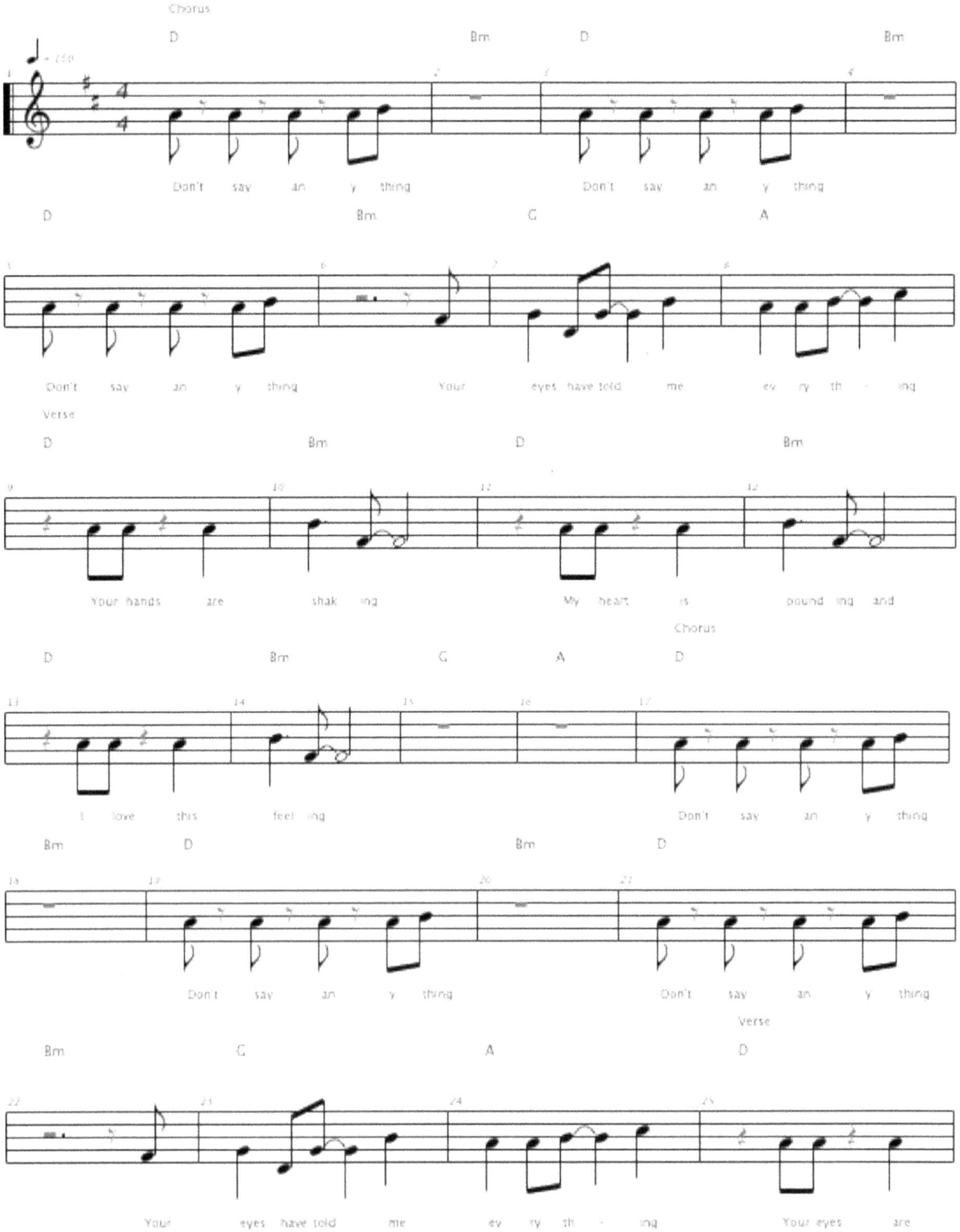

Bm · D · Bm · D · Bm

sparkling when You hear me singing and I love this feel ing

Outro

G · A · G · A · D · B

Hey hey your eyes have told me ev ry th–ing

G · A · D · B · G · A

Hey hey your eyes have told me ev ry th–ing Hey hey your

D · B · G · A · D

eyes have told me ev ry th–ing Hey hey your eyes have told me

B · G · A · D · B

ev ry th–ing

Swing

(Melody)

Gang Chen

G · · · C · · · · · · D · · · G · · · · · · G · · · · · · C · · ·

you are sit ting on a swing The swing is fly ing

G · · · D · · · G · · · · · · C · · · D · · · G

and you are smi ling and you are sit ting on a swing

I Want It All As I Have Told You

(Melody)

Gang Chen

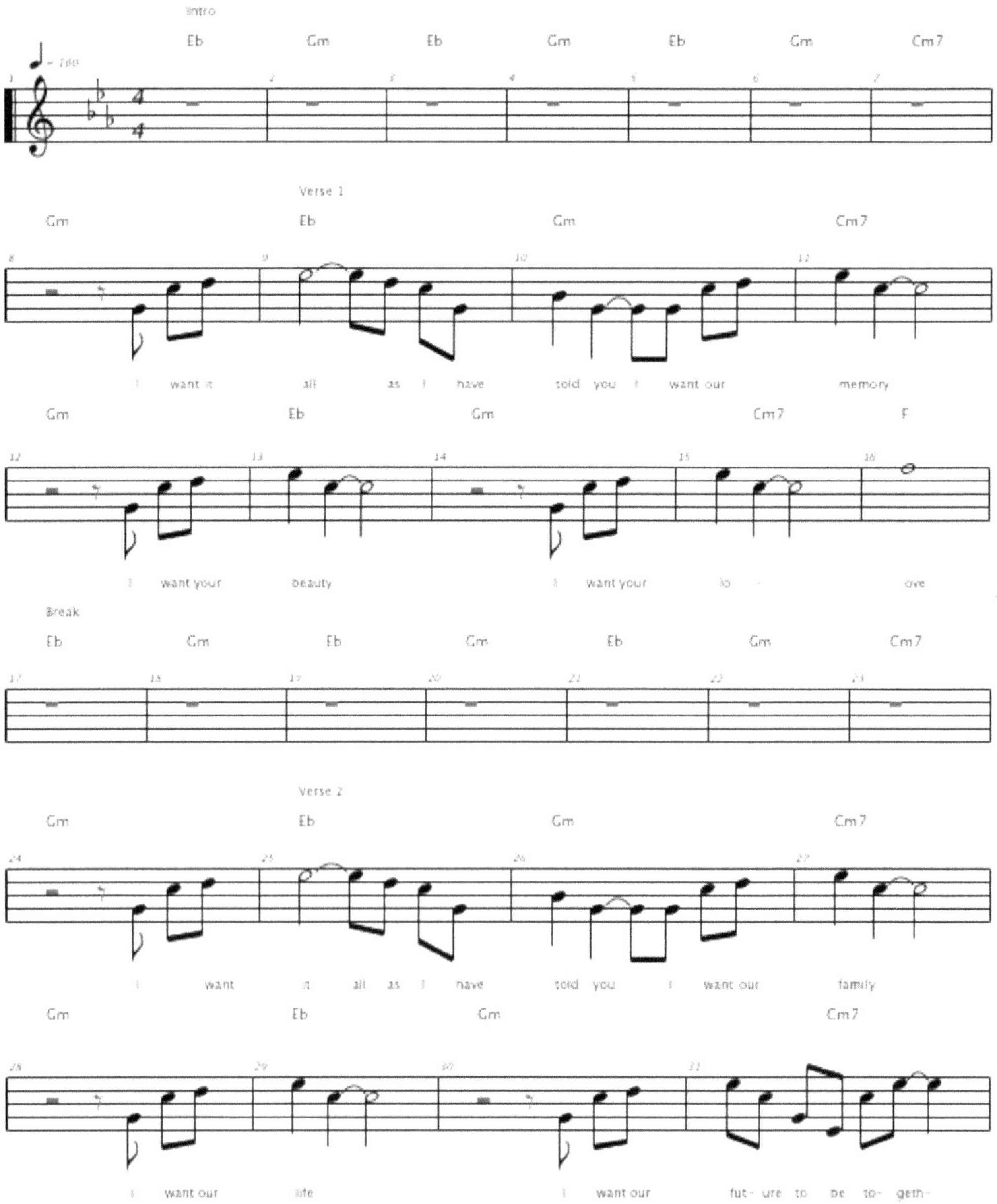

Bridge
Bb   Ab   Eb   G   Cm   Gm   G

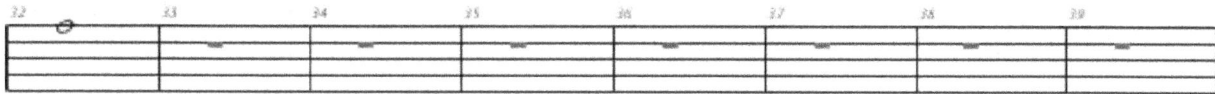

Main Line
C   E

I want it all as I have told you I want it all as I have

Am   D7

told you I want it all as I have told you I want it all as I have

G   B

told you I want it all as I have told you I want it all as I have

Em   A7

told you I want it all as I have told you I want it all as I have

D

told you I want it all as I have told you I want it

F#   Bm

all as I have told you I want it all as I have told you I want it all   as I have   told you   I want it   all   as I have

told you   I want it   all   as I have   told you   I want it   all   as I have

told you   I want it   all   as I have   told you   I want it

Appendixes

A. Frequently Asked Questions

1. **Where can I buy your singles and albums?**
   Answer: They are available at **Music.ArchiteG.com**

2. **Why should I buy your albums and singles?**
   Answer: You will like or love our albums and singles for the following simple reasons:
   1) Our albums and singles are all brand-new original songs.
   2) Our lyrics are based on true feelings and will touch your heart.
   3) Our melodies are beautiful and you'll love them.
   4) We want our melodies and lyrics to be simple and easy to remember. We follow the "KISS" principle. "KISS" stands for "Keep It Simple Stupid."
   5) Once people hear our songs for the first time, they can almost sing along or at least remember the main lines.
   6) Our singers are talented and have unique and recognizable voices. For example, our lead vocalist, Mr. Gang Chen passed several steps of a major audition in the United States, and was selected as one of the top 0.5% candidates to do live stage auditions in front of 6,128 people and four internationally acclaimed judges.
   7) Participating in various singing competition or winning them is NOT our main initiative, but just a mean to achieve our final goal. We use these competitions as a platform for people to become familiar with our songs and music.
   8) Our goal is to create hit after hit, as well as timeless and beautiful songs and music that people love. It is just a matter of time before the world knows our songs and our great singers. Our goal is to have everyone on the planet hear our songs or music. So, please help us reach our goal by spreading the word.
   9) We have been very successful with our book writing and publishing business, and our books have been the #1 bestseller in the world on green buildings for a long time now. We are starting to expand the business into song writing and music, and are working on making our music business as successful as our book publishing one. We welcome your help to achieve our goal in music.

3. **Are you going to produce albums and singles for these songs?**
   Answer: Yes. We are creating four versions of albums for these songs::
   1. **English version** (Full English vocal with background music)
   2. **Instrumental version** (Musical instrument simulating the human voice)
   3. **Karaoke version** (Background music track for Karaoke singing or sing along)
   4. **Chinese version** (Full Chinese vocal with background music)

   They are available at **Music.ArchiteG.com**

4. **How can I get permission or license to use your songs in my albums and singles?**

   Answer: You are welcome to do cover versions of our songs and use them in your own singles, albums, music video, TV shows, movies, or live performances, but you need to get our written permission or proper license first. We charge the nominal statutory rate for each license like other publishers.

   To get permission or license to use our songs, please contact us at
   info@ ArchiteG.com

   OR
   Music.ArchiteG.com
   ArchiteG.com
   GreenExamEducation.com

   We'll also use a third party agency such as Harry Fox to help us handle some of the request. See the link:
   Songfile.com

5. **How can I get translation rights for your songs?**

   Answer: Again, you are welcome to translate our songs into other languages, but you need to get our written permission or proper license first. See our contact information listed in the previous answer.

6. **Where can I buy your books?**

   Answer: They are available at **GreenExamEducation.com**

B. Major Singing Competitions

The websites for some of the major singing competitions in the United States are listed below. You can do a simple Google search to find the specific website for your country.

1. **X Factor**
   Website: **thexfactorusa.com**

2. **The Voice**
   Website: **nbc.com/the-voice**

3. **American Got Talent**
   Website: **nbc.com/americas-got-talent**

4. **American Idol**
   Website: **americanidol.com**

5. **Sing Off**
   Website: **nbc.com/sing-off**

6. **The Winner Is**
   Website: **nbc.com/the-winner-is/**